CLIMATE REPLY

TREY MOODY

CLIMATE REPLY

TREY MOODY

NEW MICHIGAN PRESS
TUCSON, ARIZONA

NEW MICHIGAN PRESS

DEPT OF ENGLISH, P. O. BOX 210067

UNIVERSITY OF ARIZONA

TUCSON, AZ 85721-0067

<http://newmichiganpress.com/nmp>

Orders and queries to nmp@thediagram.com.

Copyright © 2010 by Trey Moody.
All rights reserved.

ISBN 978-1-934832-26-4. FIRST PRINTING.

Printed in the United States of America.

Design by Ander Monson.

Cover painting, *Twenty-fourth Sunday in Ordinary Time*, courtesy of Anna Conway, 2007.

CONTENTS

What We First Said   1

The Listener, the Land   2

Climate Reply   3

Dear Ghosts

    1. Apples in the House   4

    2. Taking a Bath in Gravy   5

    3. Pinecones on the Coffee Table   6

    4. Hum of the Fridge Like Thought   7

This Forest Isn't a Room   8

The Book of Flattened Hands   9

One Question   12

The Seating   13

Dear Ghosts

    5. In the Beginning There Were Leftovers   14

    6. Like Dust around the Light Fixture   15

    7. More than Doors   16

We Didn't Believe   19

Birdsong   20

A Feather Protruding from the Mouth   21

Dear Ghosts

    8. This Time, the Fresh Paint   22

    9. So to Say the Sky   23

    10. Sam Cooke on the Radio, Alone   24

Island of Sanity 25

We Use Spoons Mostly 26

Remembering the Original 27

Acknowledgments 33

"Halfway between *cage* (cage) and *cachot* (prison cell) the French language has *cageot,* a simple openwork container for transporting fruits that sicken at the least hint of suffocation."

—Francis Ponge, "The Crate" (tr. Margaret Guiton)

WHAT WE FIRST SAID

The tiniest oak tree
                    in the tiniest room—
as we feel our eyes, our greedy joints
unhinge and root.

(The body floats, like a blue sail of surveillance.)

          In the history of human suffering,
this must be what we meant:
                    an eye or an ear,
replaced with hard clay, or a plum.

THE LISTENER, THE LAND

I ask your name to understand
who's swimming upstream. The loud knives

gleam along the forests. Sucker punch
the kidney, I tell you, bright tissue

cracks like wrapping paper,
under the lights, long forgotten by me,

my inferior raincoat. The plastic bear
rattles his plastic claws, under the chin

of his swollen prey, the green evening
casting hidden candies on benches

in hopes of understanding. I think
the meaty fish is done for, but

my flaming camp sacks have been wrong
before. The night will come again, before

this racket gets out of hand, and
in the quiet room I'll stitch

your fabric name to the tops of trees.

CLIMATE REPLY

Weather as if to repeat. Weather to read a name.
As if to ask a question, weather to strip the mane,

to feed the cats, to sleep. Go inside, weather to weep, split the maw.

Plant the plants, weather to eat the dead, their roots as if to speak.

Weather to number the names, hold the sheets
over bodies, blind as blue.   Weather as if to flame.

Scrape the storm of its howl. Cellar as if to swarm, night as if to rot.

Ground warm with flesh, ears as if to watch. Cover the eyes
with weather, weigh them down with skin.

The dead's steady hum, weather as if to win.

DEAR GHOSTS,

I. Apples in the House

In the middle of the night, when the fruit
is scariest. I hold my hand out

and I feel your nibbling. Don't worry,
my eyes are still closed. I've only

peeked that once. The cold
that is your breath—these windows

of fog. If I was outside,
I'd read your backward name again and again.

2. Taking a Bath in Gravy

Shh. Just listen—
our two bodies, coated.

If I said brown, I'd be doing
a disservice. We both

know that. I'd feed you
by the spoonful, but such

ridiculousness, to think
of a spoon! So just tell me,

like you do when I dream.
This time, don't scream.

3. Pinecones on the Coffee Table

And this won't do. One on the stove,
one under my bed sheets. You know

this just won't work. If cinnamon
smells like the hands of a baby,

then, by nightfall, I just don't want
to smell anything that's alive.

4. Hum of the Fridge Like Thought

No matter the temperature—
the banana cut in half

always turns brown. Add this
to the list. When I open the fridge

in the middle of the night, I can hear
you thinking behind me.

THIS FOREST ISN'T A ROOM

The trees are always laughing down on you.
They bare their branches—you stare at your legs.

The trees and you are different—they have water,
    continually consume.
They have trunks wider than your body.

Their trunks don't shake when they laugh, you notice.
You cannot remember what your body does

but you believe your body's not a tree, a tree not a body.
Shake with cold like you shake with cold.

The trees,
they shake their leaves like walls in the wind.

THE BOOK OF FLATTENED HANDS

This raining in my mouth is no help. The settlers outside and
                their singing of land. But the orchestra
hasn't yet come to coda and there's winter passing
            from seat to soft seat. A light from inside

your throat helps illumine this dark attic, though something violent
            happens to a lamb, which is something a grandmother spoke of
                    the week before she died, and now

the collective memory's ingrained with everything we've ever
            heard. Summer's the subject of a chain email
and may be a virus. So after years the house has swallowed the house
                and digested each and every lamp within it.

The insect under my tongue can't stop living, its body
         hard as fingernails, and the symphony's luck
has run bad, each of its arms

without strings, mouthpieces. But a body's just a body
when the light's turned out. A tiny guest bathroom:

         I can feel the shape of Japan behind my eyes.

Once, someone used the brain to discover the mouth.
         Yet the fire truck wails down the shiny street, urging
everyone: listen to the size of your existence.

The beetle can't roll over from its back
and the glass jar weighs down the counter.

A flute includes the process
             of bodily recognition—a hand covers a hand
     and skin understands its limitations. The sound of weather
crossing the Midwest brings a tear

to everyone's eye. At night
             a boy wakes up to smell his room singing
in a familiar voice. The landscape's there to remind us

of our failures, and the silence of a broken body
             brings us outside.

ONE QUESTION

The moon out, the water running,

                                     I light a candle

under your ribs.

Because I've never seen a pasture
filled with blood like bare feet.

Like dry aprons, this is not
actuality, but

                    still, the chant remains.

When the weather's right, Lord,
will I grow from the ground like a tree?

THE SEATING

Blue chair on its plastic back. Grass
and its green leaning
                         toward the dirt. More
is what we've wanted, and now—
a cue from the trees: consider the security
of your silences. Forget.
          Listen when the earth becomes self-aware
and take the red chair in your hand, set it
on the ground; sit down.

DEAR GHOSTS,

5. In the Beginning There were Leftovers

All this is to say, you still
surprise me. But it's more like fear

when it's dark. Your breath,
suddenly, on my face,

then your two big eyes!—
So at first, I would stay up and eat,

but the night was always calling me in.

6. Like Dust around the Light Fixture

So the morning came. The light bulb
didn't matter. I unscrewed it,

something as warm as flesh,
and put it in my pocket.

So you see, the days
were manageable. That is, the days

were when I missed you the most.

7. More than Doors

Have we become too
one-sided? Knock once if you believe

in structural security, twice
for mutual relationships. If I don't hear

a knock, I'll assume you're reserving
judgment, since beauty is both

conditional, subjective. Then again if I hear

nothing, my throat might well up so that
I can't speak clearly. Breathe even.

"Through thin cracks, forces from outside creep in with the cold."

—Devin Johnston, "Mouse God"

WE DIDN'T BELIEVE

Through the ceiling, where the holes were widest,
we watched the night sky

                    as it passed, placid and cold.

To each other, we burned like smooth horses.

    Though blankets were not enough, listening
pleased the violence of our ears.

Fixed to the carpet, smelled the dark grass of the fields,
bodies still warm with weather.

                        The sky a soundless face.

We've heard our mouths will taste like fire in heaven.

BIRDSONG

Night-creek waking at dawn. A simple sound to reflect the echo's width.

We waited to hear it again, and we left.

Desire to stay and demand to sleep were gone—
stones scattered aside the riverbed, though the afterthought remained:

the mud-grass and the snap-bush would have to lag behind.

To need from a structure what we've always overlooked, memory
and its silent cloud of ash—

the song was guidance, even if the pines were aware, sharing our ears.

But reason means knowing
when sound becomes the earth, its closed mouth

neglecting our grief.

And if the body precedes the compulsion of thought, then what we knew
was backward—the stone-scent of the trail depends on the trees.

The warbler claiming its loss—to find it is not enough.

The song continued, though the mind numbed.

A FEATHER PROTRUDING FROM THE MOUTH

Weather, for the moment, behind windows.
Curtains intensely made of red. This was why
we couldn't see behind them, and this was why
we didn't want to.

Light around the room fluttered with light—
wax dripped like filmed caverns.
I could still see your hand, which, for all I knew,
could've exploded any second.

Through the wall, our "hand" might've been "land,"
"sand," or "band." But it was all of these.
At the same moment you sneezed, a bird,
or something else with feathers, flew into the window.

Of course we didn't see it,
so our "flew" could've been "blue," "glue," or "God."

DEAR GHOSTS,

8. This Time, the Fresh Paint

What'd I tell you? Keep your hands off
the walls. Just remember when

I say this, I mean *please*.

9. So to Say the Sky

has left us both behind,
if I were to say, would mean

by now we share something
in common. Two footprints

in the dust. A flashlight
wanes. You know what I mean.

Both—"Your face!" and "That's not
your face." Either way, what comforts me

most is how my heart
still beats, and how somewhere,

something is listening.

10. Sam Cooke on the Radio, Alone

That's funny. But I've never heard that song
before. What a thing to do, to think

about love as something real.
When I think about you,

it reminds me of the time I sang
so loud my throat bled.

ISLAND OF SANITY

This doldrum headache—
this tremor lodged

beats a mean suitcase

made for music's swoon, but
the hand not evidently

no one's particular moon.
In this dream this

is the dream I calculate you.

WE USE SPOONS MOSTLY

What this says
about a human, as opposed to, say,
another beast, has everything to do
with electricity and warmth. Through the window

to the backyard, the river crystal-clear
like glass. Like glass? Is it human
to be redundant and to overstate
the obvious? The river, crystal-clear

between the floorboards, under
my feet, and under your feet, and the way we stand may
or may not alter its course. When was our last
rain, wasn't it Saturday, I'm pretty sure?

What memory performs as opposed to,
say, the sounds outside this window. There are
birds, and there are cicadas. There
are cicadas and there are birds and even crickets—

Hello, this moment has just recently passed.
We close our eyes more often than we think.
Let me just say, again and very quickly, one
last time, Hello.

REMEMBERING THE ORIGINAL

I saw the man standing in the field at dawn.
          He was standing like a small storm.
I looked at the sky and saw the fields coming.
Waves.   The tiny storms were on their way.

ACKNOWLEDGMENTS

Grateful thanks to the editors of the following publications where poems from this manuscript first appeared: *American Letters & Commentary* ["Climate Reply" and "Birdsong"]; *CutBank* ["One Question" and "We Didn't Believe"]; *Denver Quarterly* ["What We First Said"]; *DIAGRAM* ["The Seating"]; *Indiana Review* ["Dear Ghosts, 4" and "Dear Ghosts, 6"]; *Parcel* ["The Book of Flattened Hands"]; *past simple* ["This Forest Isn't a Room"]; *Quarterly West* ["Dear Ghosts, 1"]; *Sixth Finch* ["Dear Ghosts, 5" and "Dear Ghosts, 9"]; *Third Coast* ["The Listener, the Land"]; *Washington Square* ["We Use Spoons Mostly"]; and *Witness* ["Dear Ghosts, 10"].

Additionally, thanks to Kim Addonizio, who selected "Climate Reply" for the anthology *Best New Poets 2009*. And thanks to Katherine Fraser, whose painting, *The Director*, aided in writing "The Seating."

Thanks also to my family, friends, and teachers, especially the following who helped with these poems: Jeff Alessandrelli, Nick Courtright, Kathleen Peirce, Joshua Ware, and Steve Wilson. Most of all, thanks to my wife, Jennifer, whose caring eye and ear guided this manuscript to completion.

COLOPHON

Text is set in a digital version of Jenson, designed by Robert Slimbach in 1996, and based on the work of punchcutter, printer, and publisher Nicolas Jenson.

TREY MOODY is from Texas but lives in Nebraska.

NEW MICHIGAN PRESS, based in Tucson, Arizona, prints poetry and prose chapbooks, especially work that transcends traditional genre. Together with DIAGRAM, NMP sponsors a yearly chapbook competition.

DIAGRAM, a journal of text, art, and schematic, is published bimonthly at THEDIAGRAM.COM. Periodic print anthologies are available from the New Michigan Press at NEWMICHIGANPRESS.COM/NMP.

www.ingramcontent.com/pod-product-compliance
Lightning Source LLC
Chambersburg PA
CBHW022043050726
47591CB00003B/921